TRADING PLAN

"If you can't measure it, you can't improve it!"

Copyright 2019© Riccardo Memeo
All rights reserved
ISBN -9781096657170

Name

Surname

Date

Date
Trading instrument
Entry point
Position size
Stop-loss
Take-profit
R:R

Result   ✓ / ✗

Profit
Loss

Considerations / Trading strategy

Date
Trading instrument
Entry point
Position size
Stop-loss
Take-profit
R:R

Result ✓ / ✗

Profit
Loss

Considerations / Trading strategy

Date
Trading instrument
Entry point
Position size
Stop-loss
Take-profit
R:R

Result ✓ / ✗

Profit
Loss

Considerations / Trading strategy

Date
Trading instrument
Entry point
Position size
Stop-loss
Take-profit
R:R

Result ✓ / ✗

Profit
Loss

Considerations / Trading strategy

Date
Trading instrument
Entry point
Position size
Stop-loss
Take-profit
R:R

Result ✓ / ✗

Profit
Loss

Considerations / Trading strategy

"A goal without a plan is just a wish."
- Antoine de Saint-Exupéry -

Date
Trading instrument
Entry point
Position size
Stop-loss
Take-profit
R:R

Result ✓ / ✗

Profit
Loss

Considerations / Trading strategy

Date
Trading instrument
Entry point
Position size
Stop-loss
Take-profit
R:R

Result ✓ / ✗

Profit
Loss

Considerations / Trading strategy

Date
Trading instrument
Entry point
Position size
Stop-loss
Take-profit
R:R

Result ✓ / ✗

Profit
Loss

Considerations / Trading strategy

Date
Trading instrument
Entry point
Position size
Stop-loss
Take-profit
R:R

Result ✓ / ✗

Profit
Loss

Considerations / Trading strategy

Date
Trading instrument
Entry point
Position size
Stop-loss
Take-profit
R:R

Result ✓ / ✗

Profit
Loss

Considerations / Trading strategy

_____
_____
_____
_____
_____
_____
_____
_____
_____
_____
_____
_____

Date
Trading instrument
Entry point
Position size
Stop-loss
Take-profit
R:R

Result ✓ / ✗

Profit
Loss

Considerations / Trading strategy

Date
Trading instrument
Entry point
Position size
Stop-loss
Take-profit
R:R

Result ✓ / ✗

Profit
Loss

Considerations / Trading strategy

Date
Trading instrument
Entry point
Position size
Stop-loss
Take-profit
R:R

Result ✓ / ✗

Profit
Loss

Considerations / Trading strategy

Date
Trading instrument
Entry point
Position size
Stop-loss
Take-profit
R:R

Result ✓ / ✗

Profit
Loss

Considerations / Trading strategy

"There are no secrets to success. It is the result of preparation, hard work and learning from failure."
- Colin Powell -

Date
Trading instrument
Entry point
Position size
Stop-loss
Take-profit
R:R

Result   ✓ / ✗

Profit
Loss

Considerations / Trading strategy

Date
Trading instrument
Entry point
Position size
Stop-loss
Take-profit
R:R

Result ✓ / ✗

Profit
Loss

Considerations / Trading strategy

Date
Trading instrument
Entry point
Position size
Stop-loss
Take-profit
R:R

Result   ✓ / ✗

Profit
Loss

Considerations / Trading strategy

Date
Trading instrument
Entry point
Position size
Stop-loss
Take-profit
R:R

Result ✓ / ✗

Profit
Loss

Considerations / Trading strategy

Date
Trading instrument
Entry point
Position size
Stop-loss
Take-profit
R:R

Result ✓ / ✗

Profit
Loss

Considerations / Trading strategy

Date
Trading instrument
Entry point
Position size
Stop-loss
Take-profit
R:R

Result ✓ / ✗

Profit
Loss

Considerations / Trading strategy

Date
Trading instrument
Entry point
Position size
Stop-loss
Take-profit
R:R

Result ✓ / ✗

Profit
Loss

Considerations / Trading strategy

Date
Trading instrument
Entry point
Position size
Stop-loss
Take-profit
R:R

Result ✓ / ✗

Profit
Loss

Considerations / Trading strategy

Date
Trading instrument
Entry point
Position size
Stop-loss
Take-profit
R:R

Result ✓ / ✗

Profit
Loss

Considerations / Trading strategy

"There are two types of people who will tell you that you cannot make a difference in this world: those who are afraid to try and those who are afraid you will succeed."
- Ray Goforth -

Date
Trading instrument
Entry point
Position size
Stop-loss
Take-profit
R:R

Result ✓ / ✗

Profit
Loss

Considerations / Trading strategy

Date
Trading instrument
Entry point
Position size
Stop-loss
Take-profit
R:R

Result ✓ / ✗

Profit
Loss

Considerations / Trading strategy

Date
Trading instrument
Entry point
Position size
Stop-loss
Take-profit
R:R

Result ✓ / ✗

Profit
Loss

Considerations / Trading strategy

Date
Trading instrument
Entry point
Position size
Stop-loss
Take-profit
R:R

Result ✓ / ✗

Profit
Loss

Considerations / Trading strategy

Date
Trading instrument
Entry point
Position size
Stop-loss
Take-profit
R:R

Result ✓ / ✗

Profit
Loss

Considerations / Trading strategy

Date
Trading instrument
Entry point
Position size
Stop-loss
Take-profit
R:R

Result   ✓ / ✗

Profit
Loss

Considerations / Trading strategy

Date
Trading instrument
Entry point
Position size
Stop-loss
Take-profit
R:R

Result ✓ / ✗

Profit
Loss

Considerations / Trading strategy

Date
Trading instrument
Entry point
Position size
Stop-loss
Take-profit
R:R

Result ✓ / ✗

Profit
Loss

Considerations / Trading strategy

Date

Trading instrument

Entry point

Position size

Stop-loss

Take-profit

R:R

Result ✓ / ✗

Profit

Loss

Considerations / Trading strategy

> *"Discipline has within it the potential for creating future miracles."*
> — Jim Rohn —

Date
Trading instrument
Entry point
Position size
Stop-loss
Take-profit
R:R

Result ✓ / ✗

Profit
Loss

Considerations / Trading strategy

Date
Trading instrument
Entry point
Position size
Stop-loss
Take-profit
R:R

Result ✓ / ✗

Profit
Loss

Considerations / Trading strategy

Date
Trading instrument
Entry point
Position size
Stop-loss
Take-profit
R:R

Result ✓ / ✗

Profit
Loss

Considerations / Trading strategy

Date
Trading instrument
Entry point
Position size
Stop-loss
Take-profit
R:R

Result ✓ / ✗

Profit
Loss

Considerations / Trading strategy

Date _____
Trading instrument _____
Entry point _____
Position size _____
Stop-loss _____
Take-profit _____
R:R _____

Result ✓ / ✗

Profit _____
Loss _____

Considerations / Trading strategy

_____
_____
_____
_____
_____
_____
_____
_____
_____
_____
_____

Date
Trading instrument
Entry point
Position size
Stop-loss
Take-profit
R:R

Result ✓ / ✗

Profit
Loss

Considerations / Trading strategy

Date _____
Trading instrument _____
Entry point _____
Position size _____
Stop-loss _____
Take-profit _____
R:R _____

Result ✓ / ✗

Profit _____
Loss _____

Considerations / Trading strategy

_____
_____
_____
_____
_____
_____
_____
_____
_____
_____
_____
_____

Date
Trading instrument
Entry point
Position size
Stop-loss
Take-profit
R:R

Result   ✅ / ❌

Profit
Loss

Considerations / Trading strategy

Date
Trading instrument
Entry point
Position size
Stop-loss
Take-profit
R:R

Result ✓ / ✗

Profit
Loss

Considerations / Trading strategy

"I think if you do something and it turns out pretty good, then you should go do something else wonderful, not dwell on it for too long. Just figure out what's next."
- Steve Jobs -

Date
Trading instrument
Entry point
Position size
Stop-loss
Take-profit
R:R

Result ✓ / ✗

Profit
Loss

Considerations / Trading strategy

Date
Trading instrument
Entry point
Position size
Stop-loss
Take-profit
R:R

Result ✓ / ✗

Profit
Loss

Considerations / Trading strategy

Date
Trading instrument
Entry point
Position size
Stop-loss
Take-profit
R:R

Result ✓ / ✗

Profit
Loss

Considerations / Trading strategy

Date
Trading instrument
Entry point
Position size
Stop-loss
Take-profit
R:R

Result ✓ / ✗

Profit
Loss

Considerations / Trading strategy

Date
Trading instrument
Entry point
Position size
Stop-loss
Take-profit
R:R

Result ✓ / ✗

Profit
Loss

Considerations / Trading strategy

Date
Trading instrument
Entry point
Position size
Stop-loss
Take-profit
R:R

Result ✓ / ✗

Profit
Loss

Considerations / Trading strategy

Date
Trading instrument
Entry point
Position size
Stop-loss
Take-profit
R:R

Result ✓ / ✗

Profit
Loss

Considerations / Trading strategy

Date _____
Trading instrument _____
Entry point _____
Position size _____
Stop-loss _____
Take-profit _____
R:R _____

Result ✓ / ✗

Profit _____
Loss _____

Considerations / Trading strategy

_____
_____
_____
_____
_____
_____
_____
_____
_____
_____

Date _____
Trading instrument _____
Entry point _____
Position size _____
Stop-loss _____
Take-profit _____
R:R _____

Result ✓ / ✗

Profit _____
Loss _____

Considerations / Trading strategy

_____
_____
_____
_____
_____
_____
_____
_____
_____
_____

> *"Risk comes from not knowing what you're doing."*
> *- Warren Buffett -*

Date
Trading instrument
Entry point
Position size
Stop-loss
Take-profit
R:R

Result ✓ / ✗

Profit
Loss

Considerations / Trading strategy

Date
Trading instrument
Entry point
Position size
Stop-loss
Take-profit
R:R

Result ✓ / ✗

Profit
Loss

Considerations / Trading strategy

Date
Trading instrument
Entry point
Position size
Stop-loss
Take-profit
R:R

Result ✓ / ✗

Profit
Loss

Considerations / Trading strategy

Date
Trading instrument
Entry point
Position size
Stop-loss
Take-profit
R:R

Result ✓ / ✗

Profit
Loss

Considerations / Trading strategy

Date
Trading instrument
Entry point
Position size
Stop-loss
Take-profit
R:R

Result ✓ / ✗

Profit
Loss

Considerations / Trading strategy

Date
Trading instrument
Entry point
Position size
Stop-loss
Take-profit
R:R

Result ✓ / ✗

Profit
Loss

Considerations / Trading strategy

Date
Trading instrument
Entry point
Position size
Stop-loss
Take-profit
R:R

Result ✓ / ✗

Profit
Loss

Considerations / Trading strategy

Date
Trading instrument
Entry point
Position size
Stop-loss
Take-profit
R:R

Result ✓ / ✗

Profit
Loss

Considerations / Trading strategy

Date
Trading instrument
Entry point
Position size
Stop-loss
Take-profit
R:R

Result   ✓ / ✗

Profit
Loss

Considerations / Trading strategy

"I find that the harder I work, the more luck I seem to have."
- Thomas Jefferson -

Date
Trading instrument
Entry point
Position size
Stop-loss
Take-profit
R:R

Result   ✓ / ✗

Profit
Loss

Considerations / Trading strategy

Date
Trading instrument
Entry point
Position size
Stop-loss
Take-profit
R:R

Result ✓ / ✗

Profit
Loss

Considerations / Trading strategy

Date
Trading instrument
Entry point
Position size
Stop-loss
Take-profit
R:R

Result ✓ / ✗

Profit
Loss

Considerations / Trading strategy

Date
Trading instrument
Entry point
Position size
Stop-loss
Take-profit
R:R

Result ✓ / ✗

Profit
Loss

Considerations / Trading strategy

Date
Trading instrument
Entry point
Position size
Stop-loss
Take-profit
R:R

Result ✓ / ✗

Profit
Loss

Considerations / Trading strategy

Date
Trading instrument
Entry point
Position size
Stop-loss
Take-profit
R:R

Result ✓ / ✗

Profit
Loss

Considerations / Trading strategy

Date
Trading instrument
Entry point
Position size
Stop-loss
Take-profit
R:R

Result ✓ / ✗

Profit
Loss

Considerations / Trading strategy

Date
Trading instrument
Entry point
Position size
Stop-loss
Take-profit
R:R

Result ✓ / ✗

Profit
Loss

Considerations / Trading strategy

Date
Trading instrument
Entry point
Position size
Stop-loss
Take-profit
R:R

Result   ✓ / ✗

Profit
Loss

Considerations / Trading strategy

"Success usually comes to those who are too busy to be looking for it."
- Henry David Thoreau -

Date
Trading instrument
Entry point
Position size
Stop-loss
Take-profit
R:R

Result   ✓ / ✗

Profit
Loss

Considerations / Trading strategy

Date
Trading instrument
Entry point
Position size
Stop-loss
Take-profit
R:R

Result ✓ / ✗

Profit
Loss

Considerations / Trading strategy

Date
Trading instrument
Entry point
Position size
Stop-loss
Take-profit
R:R

Result ✓ / ✗

Profit
Loss

Considerations / Trading strategy

Date
Trading instrument
Entry point
Position size
Stop-loss
Take-profit
R:R

Result ✓ / ✗

Profit
Loss

Considerations / Trading strategy

Date
Trading instrument
Entry point
Position size
Stop-loss
Take-profit
R:R

Result ✓ / ✗

Profit
Loss

Considerations / Trading strategy

Date
Trading instrument
Entry point
Position size
Stop-loss
Take-profit
R:R

Result ✓ / ✗

Profit
Loss

Considerations / Trading strategy

Date
Trading instrument
Entry point
Position size
Stop-loss
Take-profit
R:R

Result ✓ / ✗

Profit
Loss

Considerations / Trading strategy

Date
Trading instrument
Entry point
Position size
Stop-loss
Take-profit
R:R

Result ✓ / ✗

Profit
Loss

Considerations / Trading strategy

Date
Trading instrument
Entry point
Position size
Stop-loss
Take-profit
R:R

Result   ✓ / ✗

Profit
Loss

Considerations / Trading strategy

> *"Plans are of little importance, but planning is essential."*
> — Winston Churchill —

Date
Trading instrument
Entry point
Position size
Stop-loss
Take-profit
R:R

Result   ✓ / ✗

Profit
Loss

Considerations / Trading strategy

Date
Trading instrument
Entry point
Position size
Stop-loss
Take-profit
R:R

Result ✓ / ✗

Profit
Loss

Considerations / Trading strategy

Date
Trading instrument
Entry point
Position size
Stop-loss
Take-profit
R:R

Result ✓ / ✗

Profit
Loss

Considerations / Trading strategy

Date
Trading instrument
Entry point
Position size
Stop-loss
Take-profit
R:R

Result ✓ / ✗

Profit
Loss

Considerations / Trading strategy

Date
Trading instrument
Entry point
Position size
Stop-loss
Take-profit
R:R

Result ✓ / ✗

Profit
Loss

Considerations / Trading strategy

Date
Trading instrument
Entry point
Position size
Stop-loss
Take-profit
R:R

Result   ✓ / ✗

Profit
Loss

Considerations / Trading strategy

Date
Trading instrument
Entry point
Position size
Stop-loss
Take-profit
R:R

Result   ✓ / ✗

Profit
Loss

Considerations / Trading strategy

Date
Trading instrument
Entry point
Position size
Stop-loss
Take-profit
R:R

Result ✓ / ✗

Profit
Loss

Considerations / Trading strategy

Date
Trading instrument
Entry point
Position size
Stop-loss
Take-profit
R:R

Result ✓ / ✗

Profit
Loss

Considerations / Trading strategy

> *"If you don't understand the details of your business you are going to fail."*
> *- Jeff Bezos -*

Date
Trading instrument
Entry point
Position size
Stop-loss
Take-profit
R:R

Result ✓ / ✗

Profit
Loss

Considerations / Trading strategy

Date
Trading instrument
Entry point
Position size
Stop-loss
Take-profit
R:R

Result ✓ / ✗

Profit
Loss

Considerations / Trading strategy

Date
Trading instrument
Entry point
Position size
Stop-loss
Take-profit
R:R

Result ✓ / ✗

Profit
Loss

Considerations / Trading strategy

Date _____
Trading instrument _____
Entry point _____
Position size _____
Stop-loss _____
Take-profit _____
R:R _____

Result ✓ / ✗

Profit _____
Loss _____

Considerations / Trading strategy

_____
_____
_____
_____
_____
_____
_____
_____
_____
_____
_____

Date
Trading instrument
Entry point
Position size
Stop-loss
Take-profit
R:R

Result ✓ / ✗

Profit
Loss

Considerations / Trading strategy

Date
Trading instrument
Entry point
Position size
Stop-loss
Take-profit
R:R

Result ✓ / ✗

Profit
Loss

Considerations / Trading strategy

Date
Trading instrument
Entry point
Position size
Stop-loss
Take-profit
R:R

Result ✓ / ✗

Profit
Loss

Considerations / Trading strategy

Date
Trading instrument
Entry point
Position size
Stop-loss
Take-profit
R:R

Result ✓ / ✗

Profit
Loss

Considerations / Trading strategy

Date
Trading instrument
Entry point
Position size
Stop-loss
Take-profit
R:R

Result ✓ / ✗

Profit
Loss

Considerations / Trading strategy

> *"Opportunities come infrequently. When it rains gold, put out the bucket, not the thimble"*
> *- Warren Buffett -*

Date
Trading instrument
Entry point
Position size
Stop-loss
Take-profit
R:R

Result ✓ / ✗

Profit
Loss

Considerations / Trading strategy

Date
Trading instrument
Entry point
Position size
Stop-loss
Take-profit
R:R

Result ✓ / ✗

Profit
Loss

Considerations / Trading strategy

Date
Trading instrument
Entry point
Position size
Stop-loss
Take-profit
R:R

Result ✓ / ✗

Profit
Loss

Considerations / Trading strategy

Date
Trading instrument
Entry point
Position size
Stop-loss
Take-profit
R:R

Result ✓ / ✗

Profit
Loss

Considerations / Trading strategy

Date
Trading instrument
Entry point
Position size
Stop-loss
Take-profit
R:R

Result ✓ / ✗

Profit
Loss

Considerations / Trading strategy

Date
Trading instrument
Entry point
Position size
Stop-loss
Take-profit
R:R

Result ✓ / ✗

Profit
Loss

Considerations / Trading strategy

Date
Trading instrument
Entry point
Position size
Stop-loss
Take-profit
R:R

Result ✓ / ✗

Profit
Loss

Considerations / Trading strategy

Date
Trading instrument
Entry point
Position size
Stop-loss
Take-profit
R:R

Result ✓ / ✗

Profit
Loss

Considerations / Trading strategy

Date
Trading instrument
Entry point
Position size
Stop-loss
Take-profit
R:R

Result   ✓ / ✗

Profit
Loss

Considerations / Trading strategy

"None of us can change our yesterdays but all of us can change our tomorrows."

- Colin Powell -

Date
Trading instrument
Entry point
Position size
Stop-loss
Take-profit
R:R

Result ✓ / ✗

Profit
Loss

Considerations / Trading strategy

_____
_____
_____
_____
_____
_____
_____
_____
_____
_____
_____
_____

Date
Trading instrument
Entry point
Position size
Stop-loss
Take-profit
R:R

Result   ✓ / ✗

Profit
Loss

Considerations / Trading strategy

Date
Trading instrument
Entry point
Position size
Stop-loss
Take-profit
R:R

Result   ✓ / ✗

Profit
Loss

Considerations / Trading strategy

Date
Trading instrument
Entry point
Position size
Stop-loss
Take-profit
R:R

Result ✓ / ✗

Profit
Loss

Considerations / Trading strategy

Date
Trading instrument
Entry point
Position size
Stop-loss
Take-profit
R:R

Result ✓ / ✗

Profit
Loss

Considerations / Trading strategy

Date _____
Trading instrument _____
Entry point _____
Position size _____
Stop-loss _____
Take-profit _____
R:R _____

Result ✓ / ✗

Profit _____
Loss _____

Considerations / Trading strategy

_____
_____
_____
_____
_____
_____
_____
_____
_____
_____

Date
Trading instrument
Entry point
Position size
Stop-loss
Take-profit
R:R

Result ✓ / ✗

Profit
Loss

Considerations / Trading strategy

Date
Trading instrument
Entry point
Position size
Stop-loss
Take-profit
R:R

Result   ✓ / ✗

Profit
Loss

Considerations / Trading strategy

Date
Trading instrument
Entry point
Position size
Stop-loss
Take-profit
R:R

Result ✓ / ✗

Profit
Loss

Considerations / Trading strategy

"How long should you try? Until."
- Jim Rohn -

Date
Trading instrument
Entry point
Position size
Stop-loss
Take-profit
R:R

Result ✓ / ✗

Profit
Loss

Considerations / Trading strategy

Date
Trading instrument
Entry point
Position size
Stop-loss
Take-profit
R:R

Result ✓ / ✗

Profit
Loss

Considerations / Trading strategy

Date
Trading instrument
Entry point
Position size
Stop-loss
Take-profit
R:R

Result ✓ / ✗

Profit
Loss

Considerations / Trading strategy

Date
Trading instrument
Entry point
Position size
Stop-loss
Take-profit
R:R

Result ✓ / ✗

Profit
Loss

Considerations / Trading strategy

Date
Trading instrument
Entry point
Position size
Stop-loss
Take-profit
R:R

Result ✓ / ✗

Profit
Loss

Considerations / Trading strategy

Date
Trading instrument
Entry point
Position size
Stop-loss
Take-profit
R:R

Result ✓ / ✗

Profit
Loss

Considerations / Trading strategy

Date
Trading instrument
Entry point
Position size
Stop-loss
Take-profit
R:R

Result ✓ / ✗

Profit
Loss

Considerations / Trading strategy

Date
Trading instrument
Entry point
Position size
Stop-loss
Take-profit
R:R

Result ✓ / ✗

Profit
Loss

Considerations / Trading strategy

Date
Trading instrument
Entry point
Position size
Stop-loss
Take-profit
R:R

Result ✓ / ✗

Profit
Loss

Considerations / Trading strategy

"It's not an experiment if you know it's going to work."
- Jeff Bezos -

Date
Trading instrument
Entry point
Position size
Stop-loss
Take-profit
R:R

Result ✓ / ✗

Profit
Loss

Considerations / Trading strategy

Date
Trading instrument
Entry point
Position size
Stop-loss
Take-profit
R:R

Result ✓ / ✗

Profit
Loss

Considerations / Trading strategy

Date
Trading instrument
Entry point
Position size
Stop-loss
Take-profit
R:R

Result ✓ / ✗

Profit
Loss

Considerations / Trading strategy

Date
Trading instrument
Entry point
Position size
Stop-loss
Take-profit
R:R

Result ✓ / ✗

Profit
Loss

Considerations / Trading strategy

Date
Trading instrument
Entry point
Position size
Stop-loss
Take-profit
R:R

Result ✓ / ✗

Profit
Loss

Considerations / Trading strategy

Date
Trading instrument
Entry point
Position size
Stop-loss
Take-profit
R:R

Result ✓ / ✗

Profit
Loss

Considerations / Trading strategy

Date
Trading instrument
Entry point
Position size
Stop-loss
Take-profit
R:R

Result   ✓ / ✗

Profit
Loss

Considerations / Trading strategy

Date
Trading instrument
Entry point
Position size
Stop-loss
Take-profit
R:R

Result ✓ / ✗

Profit
Loss

Considerations / Trading strategy

Date
Trading instrument
Entry point
Position size
Stop-loss
Take-profit
R:R

Result ✓ / ✗

Profit
Loss

Considerations / Trading strategy

"It is not necessary to do extraordinary things to get extraordinary results."
- Warren Buffett -

Date
Trading instrument
Entry point
Position size
Stop-loss
Take-profit
R:R

Result ✓ / ✗

Profit
Loss

Considerations / Trading strategy

Date
Trading instrument
Entry point
Position size
Stop-loss
Take-profit
R:R

Result ✓ / ✗

Profit
Loss

Considerations / Trading strategy

Date
Trading instrument
Entry point
Position size
Stop-loss
Take-profit
R:R

Result ✓ / ✗

Profit
Loss

Considerations / Trading strategy

Date
Trading instrument
Entry point
Position size
Stop-loss
Take-profit
R:R

Result ✓ / ✗

Profit
Loss

Considerations / Trading strategy

Date
Trading instrument
Entry point
Position size
Stop-loss
Take-profit
R:R

Result   ✓ / ✗

Profit
Loss

Considerations / Trading strategy

Date
Trading instrument
Entry point
Position size
Stop-loss
Take-profit
R:R

Result   ✓ / ✗

Profit
Loss

Considerations / Trading strategy

Date
Trading instrument
Entry point
Position size
Stop-loss
Take-profit
R:R

Result ✓ / ✗

Profit
Loss

Considerations / Trading strategy

Date
Trading instrument
Entry point
Position size
Stop-loss
Take-profit
R:R

Result ✓ / ✗

Profit
Loss

Considerations / Trading strategy

Date
Trading instrument
Entry point
Position size
Stop-loss
Take-profit
R:R

Result ✓ / ✗

Profit
Loss

Considerations / Trading strategy

> *"Failure Will Never Overtake Me If My Determination To Succeed Is Strong Enough."*
>
> *- Og Mandino -*

www.ingramcontent.com/pod-product-compliance
Lightning Source LLC
Chambersburg PA
CBHW070436180526
45158CB00019B/1442